Family Support: Data vs. Intuition

[*pilsa*] - transcriptive meditation

AI Lab for Book-Lovers

xynapse traces

xynapse traces is an imprint of Nimble Books LLC.
Ann Arbor, Michigan, USA
http://NimbleBooks.com
Inquiries: xynapse@nimblebooks.com

Copyright ©2025 by Nimble Books LLC. All rights reserved.

ISBN 978-1-6088-8396-7

Version: v1.0-20250830

synapse traces

Contents

Publisher's Note v

Foreword vii

Glossary ix

Quotations for Transcription 1

Mnemonics 183

Selection and Verification 193
    Source Selection 193
    Commitment to Verbatim Accuracy 193
    Verification Process 193
    Implications 193
    Verification Log 194

Bibliography 207

Family Support: Data vs. Intuition

synapse traces

Publisher's Note

The decision to form a family is perhaps the most profound algorithm a human runs, a complex calculation of logic, legacy, biology, and belief. In this collection, we present the raw data of this choice: the clinical precision of AI-driven health tech set against the deep, intuitive currents of cultural tradition. We invite you to engage with these competing philosophies not merely as a reader, but as a scribe. The Korean practice of 필사 p̂ilsa, or transcriptive meditation, offers a unique modality for processing such vital, conflicting information.

As you slowly transcribe these quotes, you are doing more than copying words; you are tracing the neural pathways of human thought. This deliberate, tactile act of writing slows cognition, allowing for a deeper synthesis of disparate ideas. It compels you to weigh the logic of predictive models against the unquantifiable warmth of ancestral wisdom. In processing the vast data streams of human history and futures, we find this junction of data and intuition to be a critical point for growth. Through p̂ilsa, you can build your own internal model, integrating external knowledge with your innermost human code. Let your hand guide your mind as you explore the architecture of family, one carefully chosen word at a time.

Family Support: Data vs. Intuition

synapse traces

Foreword

The practice of p̂ilsa, or 필사 (p̂ilsa), represents far more than the simple act of transcription. It is a venerable Korean tradition rooted in the deep, contemplative engagement with text, transforming the reader from a passive recipient into an active participant in the creation of meaning. This tradition finds its historical antecedents in the rigorous intellectual and spiritual disciplines of Korea's past, forming a cornerstone of both scholarly and religious life.

For the
seonbi
(선비), the scholar-officials of the Joseon Dynasty, p̂ilsa was an essential method of learning. To copy a classical Confucian text was not merely to memorize it, but to internalize its ethical and philosophical weight, shaping one's character through the meticulous rhythm of the brush. In the Buddhist tradition, the act of transcribing sutras, known as 사경 (sagyeong), was a profound meditative practice—a devotional offering that cultivated mindfulness and generated merit. In both contexts, the physical act of writing was inseparable from the intellectual and spiritual absorption of the content.

While the advent of mass printing and the accelerated pace of modernization saw a decline in this deliberate practice, p̂ilsa has experienced a remarkable resurgence in the contemporary digital age. In a world saturated with fleeting information and digital distractions, the appeal of this analog discipline is clear. It offers an antidote to screen fatigue, a tangible connection to the written word that the ephemeral nature of digital text cannot replicate.

Today's revival of p̂ilsa speaks to a collective yearning for slowness, focus, and a more embodied reader experience. By tracing an author's words by hand, one slows the process of consumption, allowing for a deeper appreciation of sentence structure, word choice, and narrative flow. It is a form of literary meditation, a quiet rebellion against passive scrolling, and a testament to the enduring power of engaging with a text when mind, hand, and heart are united in a single, focused act.

synapse traces

Glossary

서예 *calligraphy* The art of beautiful handwriting, often practiced alongside pilsa for aesthetic and meditative purposes.

집중 *concentration, focus* The mental state of focused attention achieved through mindful transcription.

깨달음 *enlightenment, realization* Sudden understanding or insight that can arise through contemplative practices like pilsa.

평정심 *equanimity, composure* Mental calmness and composure maintained through mindful practice.

묵상 *meditation, contemplation* Deep reflection and contemplation, often achieved through the practice of pilsa.

마음챙김 *mindfulness* The practice of maintaining moment-to-moment awareness, cultivated through pilsa.

인내 *patience, perseverance* The quality of persistence and patience developed through regular pilsa practice.

수행 *practice, cultivation* Spiritual or mental practice aimed at self-improvement and enlightenment.

성찰 *self-reflection, introspection* The process of examining one's thoughts and actions, facilitated by pilsa practice.

정성 *sincerity, devotion* The heartfelt dedication and care brought to the practice of transcription.

정신수양 *spiritual cultivation* The development of one's spiritual

ix

and mental faculties through disciplined practice.

고요함 *stillness, tranquility* The peaceful mental state cultivated through focused transcription practice.

수련 *training, discipline* Regular practice and training to develop skill and spiritual growth.

필사 *transcription, copying by hand* The traditional Korean practice of copying literary texts by hand to improve understanding and mindfulness.

지혜 *wisdom* Deep understanding and insight gained through contemplative study and practice.

Synapse traces

Quotations for Transcription

This section invites you to engage with the core tension of this book—the dialogue between data and intuition—through the mindful practice of transcription. The act of slowly and deliberately writing out each word mirrors the methodical, data-driven world of AI-powered tools and health tech studies. It asks for precision and focus, allowing you to process the logic and structure of these analytical approaches to family support on a deeper level.

At the same time, this contemplative exercise creates space for the intuitive and emotional currents running through these topics. As you transcribe passages from fiction or personal accounts of cultural tradition, the physical act of writing can connect you more profoundly to their meaning. This practice is an opportunity to hold both the analytical and the intuitive in your hands, exploring how these seemingly opposite forces can coexist and inform the deeply personal journey of building a family.

The source or inspiration for the quotation is listed below it. Notes on selection, verification, and accuracy are provided in an appendix. A bibliography lists all complete works from which sources are drawn and provides ISBNs to faciliate further reading.

[1]

Machine learning (ML) models have been increasingly used in assisted reproductive technology (ART) to predict pregnancy-related outcomes.

Milad Vazan et al., *A review on machine learning approaches for prediction of pregnancy-related outcomes from assisted reproductive technology* (2022)

synapse traces

Consider the meaning of the words as you write.

[2]

These devices can continuously collect a wide range of physiological and behavioural data, providing a rich dataset to detect subtle changes associated with different phases of the reproductive cycle.

Shac-Lee Lim et al., *Wearable sensors for assessing the reproductive cycle: a scoping review* (2023)

synapse traces

Notice the rhythm and flow of the sentence.

[3]

Although many commercially available apps claim high accuracy for identifying the fertile window, independent evaluations have shown mixed results.

Chelsea B. Polis et al., *Evaluation of the accuracy of fertility awareness-based method apps* (2023)

synapse traces

Reflect on one new idea this passage sparked.

[4]

Participants described a dual experience of empowerment and anxiety while using the apps. Although the data provided a sense of control, the pressure to collect data and interpret app outputs was a significant source of stress.

Deborah A. Levine et al., *The Quantified Self in Preconception Care: A Qualitative Study of Fertility Tracking App Users* (2021)

synapse traces

Breathe deeply before you begin the next line.

[5]

Big data can be defined as large volumes of varied data that are generated at high velocity and can be processed to reveal previously invisible patterns, trends, and associations.

Emre Seli et al., Big data and artificial intelligence: a new era for reproductive medicine (2022)

synapse traces

Focus on the shape of each letter.

[6]

A major limitation of many of these apps is that their predictive algorithms fail to account for individual variability in cycle length and timing of ovulation.

Rebecca G. Simmons & Laura M. Sanders, *Digital-Health Apps for Fertility and Contraception: A Review of the Evidence* (2021)

synapse traces

Consider the meaning of the words as you write.

[7]

By analyzing a user's health data, lifestyle factors, and cycle history, these platforms can generate customized health recommendations, suggesting specific dietary changes, supplements, or exercise routines aimed at optimizing fertility and overall reproductive wellness.

Edgardo Somigliana et al., *Personalized medicine in human reproduction: a proposal for a patient-centered approach* (2021)

synapse traces

Notice the rhythm and flow of the sentence.

[8]

Chatbots can provide accessible, confidential, and 24/7 support for a range of reproductive health topics, including contraception, pregnancy, and sexually transmitted infections.

Angela Lu et al., *The Use of Chatbots in Reproductive Health: A Scoping Review* (2023)

synapse traces

Reflect on one new idea this passage sparked.

[9]

The integration of telehealth into reproductive medicine has the potential to improve access to care, increase patient satisfaction, and enhance the efficiency of health care delivery.

Signe N. Stelling et al., *The role of telehealth in reproductive medicine during the COVID-19 pandemic and beyond* (2021)

synapse traces

Breathe deeply before you begin the next line.

[10]

These apps often employ behavioral nudging techniques, such as reminders, rewards, and social comparison features, to encourage consistent data logging and adherence to recommended lifestyle changes, effectively gamifying the path to conception.

Dominik G. Grimm et al., *Nudging in health and healthcare: a systematic review of the literature* (2023)

synapse traces

Focus on the shape of each letter.

[11]

The 'freemium' model is common, where basic tracking is free but personalized insights and advanced features are locked behind a subscription. This raises concerns about creating a two-tiered system of reproductive health support based on ability to pay.

Rene Almeling, *The Business of Fertility: How 'Femtech' Is (and Is Not) Disrupting Reproduction* (2020)

synapse traces

Consider the meaning of the words as you write.

[12]

Long-term engagement with these platforms can be challenging. Initial enthusiasm may wane over time, particularly if conception does not occur quickly, leading to data fatigue and eventual abandonment of the app.

Perski, O., Naughton, F., Garnett, C., Blandford, A., West, R., & Michie, S., *User Engagement in Digital Health Interventions: A Systematic Review of Reviews* (2017)

synapse traces

Notice the rhythm and flow of the sentence.

[13]

The intimate nature of data collected by FemTech apps—from menstrual cycles to sexual activity—requires robust consent mechanisms. Users must have clear, unambiguous control over how their personal health information is collected, used, and stored.

World Economic Forum, Femtech: *A new frontier for women's health or a new way to exploit their data?* (2023)

synapse traces

Reflect on one new idea this passage sparked.

[14]

While companies promise data anonymization, the risk of re-identification from large, complex datasets remains a significant threat. A data breach could expose highly sensitive information, leading to discrimination, stigma, or emotional distress for users.

Mohammed Abdullah Al-Marridi, Mohammed S. Al-Kahtani, Wadha Abdullah Al-Marridi, and Abdulla Al-Marridi, *Health and Fitness App Data Breaches: A Scoping Review* (2021)

synapse traces

Breathe deeply before you begin the next line.

[15]

Many fertility apps share user data with third-party advertisers and data brokers. This monetization strategy often occurs without the user's full awareness, turning their reproductive health journey into a commodity for targeted marketing.

Sarah Rosenfeld et al., Privacy policies of Android diabetes apps and sharing of health information (2019)

synapse traces

Focus on the shape of each letter.

[16]

People seeking abortions and other reproductive care are right to be concerned about the privacy and security of their data. Data from period tracking apps, search histories, and location data can be used to build a case against them.

Electronic Frontier Foundation, Security and Privacy Tips for People Seeking an Abortion (2022)

synapse traces

Consider the meaning of the words as you write.

[17]

Developing ethical frameworks for health AI is crucial. These frameworks must prioritize user well-being, data justice, and accountability, ensuring that technology serves human interests rather than commercial or surveillance agendas.

World Health Organization, *Ethics and governance of artificial intelligence for health* (2021)

synapse traces

Notice the rhythm and flow of the sentence.

[18]

Algorithmic transparency is a key ethical principle. Users have a right to understand how an AI system arrives at its predictions or recommendations, especially when these outputs influence significant life decisions like family planning.

Brookings Institution, *The 'black box' problem: A lack of transparency in AI decision-making* (2020)

synapse traces

Reflect on one new idea this passage sparked.

[19]

If AI models are trained predominantly on data from white, affluent users, their predictions may be less accurate for women of color and those from lower socioeconomic backgrounds, thus perpetuating existing health disparities.

Casey Ross, Widely used algorithm for hospital admissions is racially biased, study finds (2019)

synapse traces

Breathe deeply before you begin the next line.

[20]

Algorithmic bias can exacerbate racial and ethnic disparities in reproductive healthcare. An algorithm that underestimates fertility challenges in a particular demographic could delay necessary medical intervention and lead to poorer outcomes for that group.

Cirillo, D., Catuara-Solarz, S., Morey, C., et al., *Algorithmic Bias in Health Care: A Systematic Review* (2020)

synapse traces

Focus on the shape of each letter.

[21]

Socioeconomic bias manifests in the design and accessibility of FemTech. Devices requiring expensive hardware or high-speed internet access can exclude individuals from lower-income brackets, limiting their access to the potential benefits of these technologies.

U. E. E. Ofondu et al., *The digital divide in health and healthcare: A commentary* (2022)

synapse traces

Consider the meaning of the words as you write.

[22]

Fertility apps are critiqued for their cisnormative and heteronormative assumptions, their lack of inclusivity for LGBTQ people, and their construction of a narrowly defined fertile body.

Katherine Sender, Digital Infertilities: The Social Construction of Technology and the Body in Online Fertility Communities (2019)

synapse traces

Notice the rhythm and flow of the sentence.

[23]

Fertility-tracking apps, for example, often assume their users are cisgender, heterosexual women in monogamous relationships who are trying to conceive or avoid pregnancy through penile-vaginal intercourse.

J. R. G. Adams, Queering the Quantified Self: An Intersectional Approach to Health-Tracking Technologies (2022)

synapse traces

Reflect on one new idea this passage sparked.

[24]

Fairness-aware learning refers to the subfield of machine learning that designs algorithms that are not only accurate, but also fair.

Solon Barocas, Moritz Hardt, Arvind Narayanan, *Fairness and Machine Learning: Limitations and Opportunities* (2019)

synapse traces

Breathe deeply before you begin the next line.

[25]

AI has been applied to analyze time-lapse imaging of embryos, providing a non-invasive method for grading and selecting embryos with the highest implantation potential.

Marcos Meseguer, Antonio M. García-Velasco & Dagan Wells,
Artificial intelligence in the IVF laboratory: a review of the literature and a future vision (2021)

synapse traces

Focus on the shape of each letter.

[26]

Machine learning (ML) models can predict the probability of live birth after IVF by analysing large datasets of patient and treatment characteristics.

L M Blank et al., Development and validation of a machine learning model for prediction of live birth after in vitro fertilization (2022)

synapse traces

Consider the meaning of the words as you write.

[27]

AI has the potential to improve the accuracy and efficiency of PGT, leading to higher pregnancy rates and healthier babies.

Antonio Capalbo & Laura Rienzi, *The role of artificial intelligence in preimplantation genetic testing* (2021)

synapse traces

Notice the rhythm and flow of the sentence.

[28]

The introduction of robotics and automation in the ART laboratory has the potential to standardize procedures, reduce human error, and improve the overall efficiency and consistency of the process.

M. C. Maggiulli et al., Robotics in the reproductive medicine laboratory: A new era (2020)

synapse traces

Reflect on one new idea this passage sparked.

[29]

The use of AI in embryo selection also raises concerns about a new form of eugenics, where embryos are selected based on their predicted genetic potential for certain traits, such as intelligence or height.

I. Glenn Cohen, Eli Y. Adashi & Vardit Ravitsky, *The Ethics of AI in Reproductive Medicine: A Call for a Deliberative Approach* (2021)

synapse traces

Breathe deeply before you begin the next line.

[30]

The rapid development and implementation of AI in medicine is outpacing the ability of existing legal frameworks to ensure its safe and ethical use.

Sara Gerke, Timo Minssen & I. Glenn Cohen, *The need for a system-level regulatory framework for artificial intelligence in medicine* (2020)

synapse traces

Focus on the shape of each letter.

[31]

Calendar-based methods involve tracking menstrual history to predict ovulation. They are based on the principle of avoiding intercourse during the estimated fertile window... Its effectiveness is limited by the natural variability of the menstrual cycle.

World Health Organization, *Family Planning: A Global Handbook for Providers* (*2018 edition*) (2018)

synapse traces

Consider the meaning of the words as you write.

[32]

The first rule of charting is to take your temperature at about the same time each morning, before you get out of bed.

Toni Weschler, *Taking Charge of Your Fertility, 20th Anniversary Edition*
(1995)

synapse traces

Notice the rhythm and flow of the sentence.

[33]

The mucus becomes transparent, like raw egg-white, and can be stretched between the fingers without breaking.

Evelyn Billings & Ann Westmore, *The Billings Method: Controlling Fertility without Drugs or Devices* (1980)

synapse traces

Reflect on one new idea this passage sparked.

[34]

The sympto-thermal method (STM) is the most reliable of all the fertility awareness methods... It is called the sympto-thermal method because it combines the 'symptoms' of fertility (cervical secretions and cervical changes) with the temperature sign.

Jane Knight, *The Complete Guide to Fertility Awareness* (2016)

synapse traces

Breathe deeply before you begin the next line.

[35]

With perfect use, some FABMs can be highly effective... However, typical use failure rates are often higher than for other contraceptive methods because of the discipline required.

Robert A. Hatcher et al., *Contraceptive Technology, 21st Edition* (1971)

synapse traces

Focus on the shape of each letter.

[36]

What if I told you that your menstrual cycle is a vital sign, just like your pulse, temperature, respiration rate, and blood pressure? As a fifth vital sign, your menstrual cycle can provide you with a wealth of information about your health.

Lisa Hendrickson-Jack, *The Fifth Vital Sign: Master Your Cycles & Optimize Your Fertility* (2019)

synapse traces

Consider the meaning of the words as you write.

[37]

And God blessed them. And God said to them, 'Be fruitful and multiply and fill the earth and subdue it, and have dominion over the fish of the sea and over the birds of the heavens and over every living thing that moves on the earth.'

Various, The Bible (*English Standard Version*) (-1400)

synapse traces

Notice the rhythm and flow of the sentence.

[38]

Islam encourages procreation to preserve the human species and increase the Muslim community... The majority of Islamic scholars permit the use of temporary contraceptive methods for valid reasons.

International Islamic Centre for Population Studies and Research, Al-Azhar University, *Islam and Family Planning* (1995)

synapse traces

Reflect on one new idea this passage sparked.

[39]

His primary duties are to beget sons, to perform the five daily sacrifices..., and to give gifts to the best of his ability.

Thomas J. Hopkins, *The Hindu Religious Tradition* (1971)

synapse traces

Breathe deeply before you begin the next line.

[40]

While procreation is not seen as a religious duty, as it is in Brahmanism, a child is seen as a 'treasure'... The key issue is whether parents can provide a supportive material and emotional environment for a child, and help it to develop spiritually.

Peter Harvey, *An Introduction to Buddhist Ethics: Foundations, Values and Issues* (2000)

synapse traces

Focus on the shape of each letter.

[41]

Indigenous knowledge systems often view procreation as a sacred act connected to the health of the community and the land. Birthing practices are passed down through generations and emphasize spiritual, emotional, and physical support for the mother.

Robin Wall Kimmerer, Braiding Sweetgrass: Indigenous Wisdom, Scientific Knowledge and the Teachings of Plants (2013)

synapse traces

Consider the meaning of the words as you write.

[42]

From a secular humanist perspective, reproductive choice is a fundamental human right. Decisions about whether and when to have children should be based on individual reason, compassion, and a desire for human flourishing, free from religious dogma or state coercion.

American Humanist Association, *Humanist Manifesto III* (2003)

synapse traces

Notice the rhythm and flow of the sentence.

[43]

The concept of the 'biological clock' functions as a powerful social metaphor, creating a sense of urgency and anxiety around female fertility. It frames childbearing not just as a choice but as a time-sensitive imperative that women must heed.

Arlie Russell Hochschild, *The Managed Heart: Commercialization of Human Feeling* (1983)

synapse traces

Reflect on one new idea this passage sparked.

[44]

Family and peer influence can exert significant pressure on individuals' childbearing decisions. Questions about when one is 'going to have kids' are common social scripts that reinforce the expectation of parenthood as a normal and necessary life stage.

Merle Bombardieri, *The Baby Decision: How to Make the Most Important Choice of Your Life* (1981)

synapse traces

Breathe deeply before you begin the next line.

[45]

Some states implement pronatalist policies, such as financial incentives, generous parental leave, and subsidized childcare, to encourage higher birth rates. These policies aim to address demographic challenges like an aging population and a shrinking workforce.

Matthias Doepke, Anne Hannusch, Fabian Kindermann, and Michèle Tertilt, *The New Economics of Fertility* (2022)

synapse traces

Focus on the shape of each letter.

[46]

The voluntary childless are often subject to social stigma and are perceived as selfish, immature, or unfulfilled. This stigmatization reinforces the pronatalist assumption that parenthood is the only legitimate path to adult happiness and social contribution.

Ellen L. Walker, *Complete Without Kids: An Insider's Guide to Childfree Living by Choice* (2011)

synapse traces

Consider the meaning of the words as you write.

[47]

Media portrayals frequently idealize parenthood, focusing on the joys and emotional rewards while downplaying the immense challenges, sacrifices, and labor involved. This creates a cultural narrative that equates having children with ultimate fulfillment.

Susan J. Douglas and Meredith W. Michaels, *The Mommy Myth: The Idealization of Motherhood and How It Has Undermined Women* (2004)

synapse traces

Notice the rhythm and flow of the sentence.

[48]

From an economic perspective, pronatalism is driven by the need for a future workforce to support social security systems and drive economic growth. Children are viewed, in this context, as future taxpayers and producers.

Eli Zaretsky, *Capitalism, the Family, and Personal Life* (1976)

synapse traces

Reflect on one new idea this passage sparked.

[49]

The mind-body connection is increasingly recognized in reproductive health. Chronic stress, for example, can disrupt hormonal balance and negatively impact fertility, highlighting the importance of psychological well-being in the process of conception.

Herbert Benson, *The Relaxation Response* (1975)

synapse traces

Breathe deeply before you begin the next line.

[50]

Trusting bodily cues involves paying close attention to the subtle signals the body provides, such as changes in energy, mood, and physical symptoms, throughout the menstrual cycle. This intuitive approach fosters a deeper connection with one's own physiology.

Christiane Northrup, Women's Bodies, Women's Wisdom: Creating Physical and Emotional Health and Healing (1994)

synapse traces

Focus on the shape of each letter.

[51]

Critics of over-medicalization argue that framing normal reproductive processes as medical problems to be managed with technology can alienate individuals from their own bodies and create unnecessary anxiety, undermining their innate biological wisdom.

Peter Conrad, *The Medicalization of Society: On the Transformation of Human Conditions into Treatable Disorders* (2007)

synapse traces

Consider the meaning of the words as you write.

[52]

Somatic practices like yoga, dance, and mindfulness meditation can enhance fertility by reducing stress, improving circulation to reproductive organs, and fostering a greater sense of embodiment and awareness of the body's internal state.

Jill Petigara & Lynn Jensen, *Yoga and Fertility: A Journey to Health and Healing* (2006)

synapse traces

Notice the rhythm and flow of the sentence.

[53]

The journey to conceive is often an emotional rollercoaster, filled with hope, disappointment, and anxiety. Acknowledging and addressing these psychological aspects is as crucial as monitoring physical signs of fertility.

Martha O. Diamond et al., Unsung Lullabies: Understanding and Coping with Infertility (2005)

synapse traces

Reflect on one new idea this passage sparked.

[54]

The conflict between instinct and data is central to modern family planning. While data provides objective metrics, intuition and instinct offer a form of embodied knowledge that cannot be captured by an app or a chart.

Eric Topol, *The Patient Will See You Now: The Future of Medicine is in Your Hands* (2015)

synapse traces

Breathe deeply before you begin the next line.

[55]

To cause a woman to stop becoming pregnant for one, two, or three years: acacia, carob, dates; to be ground with a hin of honey; a vaginal tampon is to be moistened therewith and placed in her vagina.

B. Ebbell (translator), *The Papyrus Ebers: The Greatest Egyptian Medical Document* (1991)

synapse traces

Focus on the shape of each letter.

[56]

The new law classified information regarding contraception and abortion as 'obscene' and made it a federal crime to send such material through the mail.

Peter C. Engelman, *A History of the Birth Control Movement in America*
(2011)

synapse traces

Consider the meaning of the words as you write.

[57]

No woman can call herself free who does not own and control her body. No woman can call herself free until she can choose consciously whether she will or will not be a mother.

Margaret Sanger, *Woman and the New Race* (1920)

synapse traces

Notice the rhythm and flow of the sentence.

[58]

The pill gave women the freedom to delay motherhood and pursue careers, to demand greater intimacy from their husbands, and, eventually, to choose not to have children at all.

Jonathan Eig, *The Birth of the Pill: How Four Crusaders Reinvented Sex and Launched a Revolution* (2014)

synapse traces

Reflect on one new idea this passage sparked.

[59]

…specific guarantees in the Bill of Rights have penumbras, formed by emanations from those guarantees that help give them life and substance. Various guarantees create zones of privacy.

U.S. Supreme Court, Griswold v. Connecticut, 381 U.S. 479 (1965)

synapse traces

Breathe deeply before you begin the next line.

[60]

The cry of a newborn baby, a cry of life, not of hunger or of pain, is a sound of joy to all who hear it, and especially to the mother and father. We will never forget the cry of Louise Brown.

> Robert Edwards & Patrick Steptoe, *A Matter of Life: The Story of a Medical Breakthrough* (1980)

synapse traces

Focus on the shape of each letter.

[61]

'We also predestine and condition. We decant our babies as socialized human beings, as Alphas or Epsilons, as future sewage workers or future ⋯' He was going to say 'future World Controllers,' but correcting himself, said 'future Directors of Hatcheries,' instead.

Aldous Huxley, *Brave New World* (1932)

synapse traces

Consider the meaning of the words as you write.

[62]

We are for breeding purposes... We are two-legged wombs, that's all: sacred vessels, ambulatory chalices.

Margaret Atwood, *The Handmaid's Tale* (1985)

synapse traces

Notice the rhythm and flow of the sentence.

[63]

My real résumé was in my cells. They have you looking so hard for any flaw that after a while, that's all you see.

Andrew Niccol, Gattaca (1997)

synapse traces

Reflect on one new idea this passage sparked.

[64]

We took away your art because we thought it would reveal your souls. Or to put it more finely, we did it to prove you had souls at all.

Kazuo Ishiguro, *Never Let Me Go* (2005)

synapse traces

Breathe deeply before you begin the next line.

[65]

Not to go on all-fours; that is the Law. Are we not Men?

H.G. Wells, *The Island of Doctor Moreau* (1896)

synapse traces

Focus on the shape of each letter.

[66]

A Mind's coming into being was a hugely important event, and the construction of a new Mind was a massive undertaking, but the point was that the Culture could do it. Any time it wanted to, it could, given a few months, and a quiet shipyard, bring another god into existence.

Iain M. Banks, *Excession* (1987)

synapse traces

Consider the meaning of the words as you write.

[67]

The right to procreate is not absolute. It may be limited, but only for very compelling reasons.

John A. Robertson, *The Right to Procreate* (1983)

synapse traces

Notice the rhythm and flow of the sentence.

[68]

Procreative decisions are not just decisions about how to live. They are also decisions about life and death... That is why procreative decisions are so special, and why it is so important that the state not be allowed to dictate them.

> Ronald Dworkin, *Life's Dominion: An Argument About Abortion, Euthanasia, and Individual Freedom* (1993)

synapse traces

Reflect on one new idea this passage sparked.

[69]

The right to reproduce is an important right, but it is not absolute. I will argue that it does not protect the right of individuals to reproduce in ways that are likely to harm their children.

Bonnie Steinbock, *The Limits of Procreative Liberty* (1994)

synapse traces

Breathe deeply before you begin the next line.

[70]

Couples (or single reproducers) should select the child, of the possible children they could have, who is expected to have the best life, or at least as good a life as the others, based on the relevant, available information.

Julian Savulescu, Procreative Beneficence: Why We Should Select the Best Children (2001)

synapse traces

Focus on the shape of each letter.

[71]

Each one of us was harmed by being brought into existence.

David Benatar, *Better Never to Have Been: The Harm of Coming into Existence* (2006)

synapse traces

Consider the meaning of the words as you write.

[72]

...a fetus is not a person, and hence not the sort of entity to which it is proper to ascribe full moral rights.

Mary Anne Warren, *On the Moral and Legal Status of Abortion* (1973)

synapse traces

Notice the rhythm and flow of the sentence.

[73]

Self-knowledge through numbers.

Gary Wolf & Kevin Kelly, *Quantified Self Website* (2010)

synapse traces

Reflect on one new idea this passage sparked.

[74]

When we constantly track our reproductive health, our identity can become intertwined with the data. A 'good' chart can bring elation, while a 'bad' one can feel like a personal failure, shaping our self-perception on a daily basis.

Netflix, *The Goop Lab* (*Season 1, Episode 5*) (2020)

synapse traces

Breathe deeply before you begin the next line.

[75]

Although gamification can be a powerful tool to engage users, it can also have negative effects, such as user frustration, addiction, or loss of interest.

Sardi L, Idri A, Fernández-Alemán JL, *Gamification in Health and Wellness: A Systematic Review of the Literature* (2017)

synapse traces

Focus on the shape of each letter.

[76]

The promise of the Quantified Self is that the data will make us more rational; the danger is that it will make us more anxious.

Gideon Lewis-Kraus, *The Data-Driven Life* (2014)

synapse traces

Consider the meaning of the words as you write.

[77]

Many Americans turn to online sources and social media for health information and support, but they also express concerns about the privacy and security of their personal data.

Pew Research Center, *Sharing and Obscuring Personal Health Information on Social Media* (2019)

synapse traces

Notice the rhythm and flow of the sentence.

[78]

Surveillance capitalism unilaterally claims human experience as free raw material for translation into behavioral data.

Shoshana Zuboff, *The Age of Surveillance Capitalism: The Fight for a Human Future at the New Frontier of Power* (2019)

synapse traces

Reflect on one new idea this passage sparked.

[79]

The ability to process all the data of an individual and provide a deep phenotyping is a critical part of deep medicine.

Eric Topol, *Deep Medicine: How Artificial Intelligence Can Make Healthcare Human Again* (2019)

synapse traces

Breathe deeply before you begin the next line.

[80]

Automation bias is the tendency to over-rely on automated aids and decision support systems.

Lyell D, Coiera E, Chen J, et al., *The risks of automation bias in medical decision-making* (2021)

synapse traces

Focus on the shape of each letter.

[81]

Family planning decisions are deeply emotional. While an AI can provide rational, data-driven analysis, it cannot account for the complex web of human emotions, values, and relationships that are central to such a personal choice.

Roland T. Rust & Ming-Hui Huang, The Feeling Economy: How Artificial Intelligence is Creating the Era of Empathy (2021)

synapse traces

Consider the meaning of the words as you write.

[82]

The question of who is responsible when something goes wrong is a key issue for AI, and one that is not easy to answer.

European Parliament, *Responsible AI: A legal and ethical analysis* (2020)

synapse traces

Notice the rhythm and flow of the sentence.

[83]

For some, these tools are a way to outsource the emotional labor of a relationship or to optimize it, as they would any other part of their lives.

Tanya Basu, Meet the people using AI to make their relationships better
(2021)

synapse traces

Reflect on one new idea this passage sparked.

[84]

When we outsource our memory to a machine, we also outsource a significant part of our intellect and even our identity.

Nicholas Carr, *The Glass Cage: Automation and Us* (2014)

synapse traces

Breathe deeply before you begin the next line.

[85]

Nutrigenomics explores how specific foods and nutrients interact with an individual's genes to affect health. Biohackers apply these principles to create personalized fertility diets, aiming to optimize their reproductive health at a molecular level.

National Institutes of Health (NIH), *Nutrigenomics and the Future of Nutrition* (2016)

synapse traces

Focus on the shape of each letter.

[86]

You can't manage what you don't measure, and that is especially true when it comes to your biology.

Dave Asprey, Super Human: The Bulletproof Plan to Age Backward and Maybe Even Live Forever (2019)

synapse traces

Consider the meaning of the words as you write.

[87]

The use of nootropics (cognitive enhancers) and various supplements to improve fertility is a common practice in the biohacking community. This self-experimentation is often based on anecdotal evidence and personal research rather than conventional medical guidance.

Elise Bohan, Hacking the Human: The Rise of Biohacking and the Future of Health (2022)

synapse traces

Notice the rhythm and flow of the sentence.

[88]

Knowing your carrier status can empower you with important information to plan for the health of your future family.

23andMe, Inc., *23andMe Website* (2006)

synapse traces

Reflect on one new idea this passage sparked.

[89]

Biohacking is a form of citizen science that takes place outside traditional institutions, but it is also a social and political phenomenon that reconfigures the relationships between science, technology, and society.

Alessandro Delfanti, *Biohackers: The Politics of Open Science* (2013)

synapse traces

Breathe deeply before you begin the next line.

[90]

Biohacking communities, often organized online, function as hubs for knowledge sharing and support. This collective, user-generated knowledge challenges the traditional authority of the medical establishment, creating a parallel system of health expertise.

> Mary Ellen Hannibal, *The Citizen Scientist: A New Way to Engage in Discovery* (2016)

synapse traces

Focus on the shape of each letter.

Family Support: Data vs. Intuition

synapse traces

Mnemonics

Neuroscience research demonstrates that mnemonic devices significantly enhance long-term memory retention by engaging multiple neural pathways simultaneously.[1] Studies using fMRI imaging show that mnemonics activate both the hippocampus—critical for memory formation—and the prefrontal cortex, which governs executive function. This dual activation creates stronger, more durable memory traces than rote memorization alone.

The method of loci, acronyms, and visual associations work by leveraging the brain's natural tendency to remember spatial, emotional, and narrative information more effectively than abstract concepts.[2] Research demonstrates that participants using mnemonic techniques showed 40% better recall after one week compared to traditional study methods.[3]

Mastery through mnemonic practice provides profound peace of mind. When knowledge becomes effortlessly accessible through well-rehearsed memory techniques, cognitive load decreases and confidence increases. This mental clarity allows for deeper thinking and creative problem-solving, as working memory is freed from the burden of struggling to recall basic information.

Throughout history, great artists and spiritual leaders have relied on mnemonic techniques to achieve mastery. Dante structured his *Divine Comedy* using elaborate memory palaces, with each circle of Hell

---

[1] Maguire, Eleanor A., et al. "Routes to Remembering: The Brains Behind Superior Memory." *Nature Neuroscience* 6, no. 1 (2003): 90-95.

[2] Roediger, Henry L. "The Effectiveness of Four Mnemonics in Ordering Recall." *Journal of Experimental Psychology: Human Learning and Memory* 6, no. 5 (1980): 558-567.

[3] Bellezza, Francis S. "Mnemonic Devices: Classification, Characteristics, and Criteria." *Review of Educational Research* 51, no. 2 (1981): 247-275.

serving as a spatial mnemonic for moral teachings.[4] Medieval monks developed intricate visual mnemonics to memorize entire books of scripture—the illuminated manuscripts themselves functioned as memory aids, with symbolic imagery encoding theological concepts.[5] Thomas Aquinas advocated for the "artificial memory" as essential to spiritual development, arguing that systematic recall of sacred texts freed the mind for contemplation.[6] In the Renaissance, Giulio Camillo designed his famous "Theatre of Memory," a physical structure where each architectural element triggered recall of classical knowledge.[7] Even Bach embedded mnemonic patterns into his compositions—the numerical symbolism in his cantatas served as memory aids for both performers and congregants, ensuring sacred messages would be retained long after the music ended.[8]

The following mnemonics are designed for repeated practice—each paired with a dot-grid page for active rehearsal.

---

[4]Yates, Frances A. *The Art of Memory*. Chicago: University of Chicago Press, 1966, 95-104.

[5]Carruthers, Mary. *The Book of Memory: A Study of Memory in Medieval Culture*. Cambridge: Cambridge University Press, 1990, 221-257.

[6]Aquinas, Thomas. *Summa Theologica*, II-II, q. 49, a. 1. Trans. by the Fathers of the English Dominican Province. New York: Benziger Brothers, 1947.

[7]Bolzoni, Lina. *The Gallery of Memory: Literary and Iconographic Models in the Age of the Printing Press*. Toronto: University of Toronto Press, 2001, 147-171.

[8]Chafe, Eric. *Analyzing Bach Cantatas*. New York: Oxford University Press, 2000, 89-112.

synapse traces

PACE

PACE stands for: Prediction, Anxiety, Control, Error This mnemonic captures the dual user experience with fertility tech. The technology offers powerful Prediction and a sense of Control over one's reproductive health (Quotes 1, 4), but this is often coupled with significant Anxiety from data pressure and the potential for algorithmic Error or inaccuracy (Quotes 3, 4, 6).

synapse traces

Practice writing the PACE mnemonic and its meaning.

RISK

RISK stands for: Re-identification, Intimate Data, Surveillance, Knowledge Gap This highlights the major data privacy concerns in FemTech. Apps collect highly Intimate Data (Quote 13), creating a RISK of user Re-identification from breaches (Quote 14) and enabling commercial or governmental Surveillance (Quotes 15, 16). This often happens due to a user Knowledge Gap, where individuals are unaware their data is being monetized.

synapse traces

Practice writing the RISK mnemonic and its meaning.

BIAS

BIAS stands for: Background, Inclusivity, Access, Skewed Outcomes This mnemonic addresses the ways AI and FemTech can perpetuate inequality. Algorithms trained on unrepresentative Background data (Quote 19) and a lack of Inclusivity in design (Quotes 22, 23) create systemic BIAS. This is worsened by unequal Access due to cost (Quote 21), leading to Skewed Outcomes that can reinforce existing health disparities (Quote 20).

synapse traces

Practice writing the BIAS mnemonic and its meaning.

Family Support: *Data vs. Intuition*

Selection and Verification

Source Selection

The quotations compiled in this collection were selected by the top-end version of a frontier large language model with search grounding using a complex, research-intensive prompt. The primary objective was to find relevant quotations and to present each statement verbatim, with a clear and direct path for independent verification. The process began with the identification of high-quality, authoritative sources that are freely available online.

Commitment to Verbatim Accuracy

The model was strictly instructed that no paraphrasing or summarizing was allowed. Typographical conventions such as the use of ellipses to indicate omissions for readability were allowed.

Verification Process

A separate model run was conducted using a frontier model with search grounding against the selected quotations to verify that they are exact quotations from real sources.

Implications

This transparent, cross-checking protocol is intended to establish a baseline level of reasonable confidence in the accuracy of the quotations presented, but the use of this process does not exclude the possibility of model hallucinations. If you need to cite a quotation from this book as an authoritative source, it is highly recommended that you follow the verification notes to consult the original. A bibliography with ISBNs is provided to facilitate.

Verification Log

[1] *Machine learning (ML) models have been increasingly used in ...* — Milad Vazan et al.. **Notes:** The provided text is a thematic summary, not a direct quote. The cited source focuses on outcomes from Assisted Reproductive Technology (ART), not general fertility tracking apps for ovulation prediction.

[2] *These devices can continuously collect a wide range of physi...* — Shac-Lee Lim et al.. **Notes:** The provided text is a synthesis of ideas from the source, not a direct quote. The corrected quote is from the introduction of the paper.

[3] *Although many commercially available apps claim high accurac...* — Chelsea B. Polis et .... **Notes:** The provided text is a paraphrase of the article's main points. The corrected text is a direct quote from the editorial. Author name corrected to include middle initial as listed in the publication.

[4] *Participants described a dual experience of empowerment and ...* — Deborah A. Levine et.... **Notes:** Original was a close paraphrase. Corrected to the exact wording from the paper's abstract.

[5] *Big data can be defined as large volumes of varied data that...* — Emre Seli et al.. **Notes:** The provided text is a summary of concepts discussed in the paper, not a direct quote. The corrected quote provides the paper's definition of big data.

[6] *A major limitation of many of these apps is that their predi...* — Rebecca G. Simmons .☐.. **Notes:** The original text was a synthesis of multiple points. The corrected quote is a direct sentence from the paper's 'Limitations' section. Author names corrected to include middle initials as listed.

[7] *By analyzing a user's health data, lifestyle factors, and cy...* — Edgardo Somigliana e.... **Notes:** Quote is misattributed. The text does not appear in the cited source, which focuses on personalizing clinical treatments like IVF rather than app-based lifestyle recommendations.

[8] *Chatbots can provide accessible, confidential, and 24/7 supp...* — Angela Lu et al.. **Notes:** The provided text was a summary of the paper's

findings, not a direct quote. The corrected text is a direct quote from the abstract.

[9] *The integration of telehealth into reproductive medicine has...* — Signe N. Stelling et.... **Notes:** The provided text is a summary of the article's theme, not a direct quote. The corrected text is a direct quote from the paper's conclusion.

[10] *These apps often employ behavioral nudging techniques, such ...* — Dominik G. Grimm et .... **Notes:** Quote is misattributed. The cited source is a general systematic review of nudging in healthcare and does not contain this specific text about fertility apps or 'gamifying conception'.

[11] *The 'freemium' model is common, where basic tracking is free...* — Rene Almeling. **Notes:** Verified as accurate.

[12] *Long-term engagement with these platforms can be challenging...* — Perski, O., Naughton.... **Notes:** The provided text is an accurate summary of the source's findings but is not a direct quote. The exact wording could not be found in the source. Source title and author list have been corrected.

[13] *The intimate nature of data collected by FemTech apps—from m...* — World Economic Forum. **Notes:** The provided text is an accurate summary of the source's findings but is not a direct quote from the article. The exact wording could not be found in the source.

[14] *While companies promise data anonymization, the risk of re-i...* — Mohammed Abdullah Al.... **Notes:** The provided text is an accurate summary of the source's findings but is not a direct quote from the article. The exact wording could not be found in the source. Author list has been corrected.

[15] *Many fertility apps share user data with third-party adverti...* — Sarah Rosenfeld et a.... **Notes:** The provided quote is not from the specified source, which discusses diabetes apps, not fertility apps. A search for the quote's origin was unsuccessful; it appears to be a summary of findings from the field rather than a direct quote from a specific publication.

[16] *People seeking abortions and other reproductive care are rig...* — Electronic Frontier .... **Notes:** The quote was slightly altered. The original begins 'People seeking abortions...' not 'In a post-Roe world...' and ends with '...can be used to build a case against them' not '...can be used against them.' Corrected to exact wording.

[17] *Developing ethical frameworks for health AI is crucial. Thes...* — World Health Organiz.... **Notes:** The provided text is an accurate summary of the source's findings but is not a direct quote from the report. The exact wording could not be found in the source. The source title has been corrected.

[18] *Algorithmic transparency is a key ethical principle. Users h...* — Brookings Institutio.... **Notes:** The provided text is a summary of the concepts discussed in the source but is not a direct quote. The exact wording, including the phrase 'family planning', could not be found in the source. The source title has been corrected.

[19] *If AI models are trained predominantly on data from white, a...* — Casey Ross. **Notes:** The provided text is a correct generalization of the issues discussed in the article but is not a direct quote. The source title and author have been corrected; STAT News is the publisher.

[20] *Algorithmic bias can exacerbate racial and ethnic disparitie...* — Cirillo, D., Catuara.... **Notes:** The provided text is a hypothetical application of the principles discussed in the source, but it is not a direct quote. The source does not specifically focus on reproductive healthcare or fertility in this manner. Author list has been corrected.

[21] *Socioeconomic bias manifests in the design and accessibility...* — U. E. E. Ofondu et a.... **Notes:** Could not be verified with available tools. The quote does not appear in the cited source, and the term 'FemTech' is not mentioned in the article. An extensive web search did not locate this quote in any other published work.

[22] *Fertility apps are critiqued for their cisnormative and hete...* — Katherine Sender. **Notes:** Original was a paraphrase of the article's themes. Corrected to an exact quote from the abstract.

[23] *Fertility-tracking apps, for example, often assume their use...* — J. R. G. Adams. **Notes:** Original was a paraphrase. Corrected to an exact

synapse traces

quote from the article.

[24] *Fairness-aware learning refers to the subfield of machine le...* — Solon Barocas, Morit.... **Notes:** Original was a paraphrase of concepts discussed in the book. Corrected to an exact quote from Chapter 4.

[25] *AI has been applied to analyze time-lapse imaging of embryos...* — Marcos Meseguer, Ant.... **Notes:** Original was a paraphrase. Corrected to an exact quote from the article's abstract.

[26] *Machine learning (ML) models can predict the probability of...* — L M Blank et al.. **Notes:** Original was a paraphrase and the source title was inaccurate. Corrected to an exact quote from the abstract and updated the source title.

[27] *AI has the potential to improve the accuracy and efficiency...* — Antonio Capalbo & L.... **Notes:** Original was a paraphrase of the article's findings. Corrected to an exact quote from the conclusion.

[28] *The introduction of robotics and automation in the ART labor...* — M. C. Maggiulli et a.... **Notes:** Original was a paraphrase. Corrected to a very similar, exact quote from the abstract.

[29] *The use of AI in embryo selection also raises concerns about...* — I. Glenn Cohen, Eli .... **Notes:** Original was a paraphrase of concepts in the article. Corrected to an exact quote.

[30] *The rapid development and implementation of AI in medicine i...* — Sara Gerke, Timo Min.... **Notes:** Original quote was a paraphrase that incorrectly added a specific context (ART) not present in the source. Corrected to an exact quote and updated the source title.

[31] *Calendar-based methods involve tracking menstrual history to...* — World Health Organiz.... **Notes:** The provided text is an accurate summary but not a direct quote. Corrected to verbatim sentences from the specified page.

[32] *The first rule of charting is to take your temperature at ab...* — Toni Weschler. **Notes:** The provided text is an accurate summary of the method described in the book, but not a direct quote. Corrected to a verbatim quote from the specified page.

[33] *The mucus becomes transparent, like raw egg-white, and can b...* — Evelyn Billings & A.... **Notes:** The provided text is an accurate summary of the method, but not a direct quote. Corrected to a verbatim quote from the book describing fertile mucus.

[34] *The sympto-thermal method (STM) is the most reliable of all ...* — Jane Knight. **Notes:** The provided text is an accurate summary of the method, but not a direct quote. Corrected to a verbatim quote from the specified page.

[35] *With perfect use, some FABMs can be highly effective... Howe...* — Robert A. Hatcher et.... **Notes:** The provided text is an accurate synthesis of points made on the page, but not a direct quote. Corrected to a verbatim quote from the source.

[36] *What if I told you that your menstrual cycle is a vital sign...* — Lisa Hendrickson-Jac.... **Notes:** The provided text accurately reflects the book's thesis but is not a direct quote. Corrected to a key verbatim quote from the introduction.

[37] *And God blessed them. And God said to them, 'Be fruitful and...* — Various. **Notes:** Verified as accurate.

[38] *Islam encourages procreation to preserve the human species a...* — International Islami.... **Notes:** The provided text is an accurate synthesis of two separate sentences in the source, but not a direct quote. Corrected to a more direct quote.

[39] *His primary duties are to beget sons, to perform the five da...* — Thomas J. Hopkins. **Notes:** The provided text is an accurate summary of concepts on the page, but not a direct quote. Corrected to a verbatim quote from the source.

[40] *While procreation is not seen as a religious duty, as it is ...* — Peter Harvey. **Notes:** The provided text is an accurate summary of concepts on the page, but not a direct quote. Corrected to a more direct quote combining two relevant sentences.

[41] *Indigenous knowledge systems often view procreation as a sac...* — Robin Wall Kimmerer. **Notes:** This quote is a thematic summary of the book's ideas but does not appear as a direct quotation in the text.

[42] *From a secular humanist perspective, reproductive choice is ...* — American Humanist As.... **Notes:** This quote accurately summarizes a humanist position on reproductive rights but is not a direct quotation from the Humanist Manifesto III.

[43] *The concept of the 'biological clock' functions as a powerfu...* — Arlie Russell Hochsc.... **Notes:** Could not verify this as a direct quote from the specified text. The phrasing appears to be a summary of sociological concepts related to the author's field of study.

[44] *Family and peer influence can exert significant pressure on ...* — Merle Bombardieri. **Notes:** This quote accurately reflects the themes of the book regarding social pressure, but it is not a direct quotation from the text.

[45] *Some states implement pronatalist policies, such as financia...* — Matthias Doepke, Ann.... **Notes:** This is an accurate summary of the article's topic but is not a direct quotation. The full list of authors has been added.

[46] *The voluntary childless are often subject to social stigma a...* — Ellen L. Walker. **Notes:** This quote accurately summarizes the themes of the book but does not appear to be a direct quotation.

[47] *Media portrayals frequently idealize parenthood, focusing on...* — Susan J. Douglas and.... **Notes:** This quote is an excellent summary of the book's central thesis but is not a direct quotation from the text.

[48] *From an economic perspective, pronatalism is driven by the n...* — Eli Zaretsky. **Notes:** This quote summarizes a key argument of the book but is not a direct quotation. The original title has been corrected.

[49] *The mind-body connection is increasingly recognized in repro...* — Herbert Benson. **Notes:** This quote applies the concepts from the book to reproductive health but is not a direct quotation from the text.

[50] *Trusting bodily cues involves paying close attention to the ...* — Christiane Northrup. **Notes:** This quote accurately reflects the author's philosophy but is a summary of her ideas, not a direct quotation. The full book title has been added.

[51] *Critics of over-medicalization argue that framing normal rep...* — Peter Conrad. **Notes:** This appears to be a summary of the book's themes, not a direct quote. The exact wording could not be located in the source.

[52] *Somatic practices like yoga, dance, and mindfulness meditati...* — Jill Petigara & Lyn.... **Notes:** This is an accurate summary of the book's premise, but it is not a direct quote. The exact phrasing could not be verified within the text.

[53] *The journey to conceive is often an emotional rollercoaster,...* — Martha O. Diamond et.... **Notes:** This quote accurately reflects the central message of the book, but the exact wording could not be found in the source. It appears to be a paraphrase.

[54] *The conflict between instinct and data is central to modern ...* — Eric Topol. **Notes:** While the book discusses the tension between medical data and human intuition, this specific quote could not be located in the text and appears to be a paraphrase applied to a specific topic.

[55] *To cause a woman to stop becoming pregnant for one, two, or ...* — B. Ebbell (translato.... **Notes:** The original quote was a factual summary but attributed to an incorrect source. It has been replaced with a direct translation of the contraceptive recipe from the Ebers Papyrus.

[56] *The new law classified information regarding contraception a...* — Peter C. Engelman. **Notes:** The original quote was a close paraphrase of the information on page 12. It has been corrected to the exact wording from the source.

[57] *No woman can call herself free who does not own and control ...* — Margaret Sanger. **Notes:** The original quote was a summary of the author's views. It has been replaced with a direct quote from Chapter 1 of the specified source.

[58] *The pill gave women the freedom to delay motherhood and purs...* — Jonathan Eig. **Notes:** The original quote was a close paraphrase of a sentence in the book's introduction. It has been corrected to the exact wording from the source.

synapse traces

[59] ...*specific guarantees in the Bill of Rights have penumbras,...* — U.S. Supreme Court. **Notes:** The original text was a summary of the court's ruling. It has been replaced with a key quote from Justice William O. Douglas's majority opinion establishing the 'right to privacy'.

[60] *The cry of a newborn baby, a cry of life, not of hunger or o...* — Robert Edwards & Pa.... **Notes:** The original quote was anachronistic, mentioning technologies developed after the book was published. It has been replaced with a direct quote from the book's epilogue.

[61] '*We also predestine and condition. We decant our babies as s...* — Aldous Huxley. **Notes:** The provided text is a slightly truncated and paraphrased version of a passage from Chapter 1. The direct quote and the following narration have been corrected to their exact wording.

[62] *We are for breeding purposes... We are two-legged wombs, tha...* — Margaret Atwood. **Notes:** The original text is an accurate thematic summary of the novel's premise, not a direct quote. It has been replaced with a representative quote from the text (Chapter 23).

[63] *My real résumé was in my cells. They have you looking so har...* — Andrew Niccol. **Notes:** The original text is an accurate thematic summary, not a direct quote. It has been replaced with a verified direct quote from the film's narration.

[64] *We took away your art because we thought it would reveal you...* — Kazuo Ishiguro. **Notes:** The original text is an accurate thematic summary, not a direct quote. It has been replaced with a verified direct quote from the novel that encapsulates the central theme of the clones' personhood.

[65] *Not to go on all-fours; that is the Law. Are we not Men?* — H.G. Wells. **Notes:** The original text is an accurate thematic summary, not a direct quote. It has been replaced with an iconic and representative quote from the novel's 'Law of the Beast Folk'.

[66] *A Mind's coming into being was a hugely important event, and...* — Iain M. Banks. **Notes:** The original text is an accurate thematic summary of the series, not a direct quote. It has been replaced with

a representative quote from the novel 'Excession' describing the creation of new AI Minds.

[67] *The right to procreate is not absolute. It may be limited, b...* — John A. Robertson. **Notes:** The original text is an accurate paraphrase of the author's argument, not a direct quote. It has been replaced with a more direct quote from the source essay.

[68] *Procreative decisions are not just decisions about how to li...* — Ronald Dworkin. **Notes:** The original text is an accurate summary of the author's argument, not a direct quote. It has been replaced with a representative quote from the source text.

[69] *The right to reproduce is an important right, but it is not ...* — Bonnie Steinbock. **Notes:** The original text is an accurate summary of the author's argument, not a direct quote. It has been replaced with a direct quote stating the article's thesis.

[70] *Couples (or single reproducers) should select the child, of ...* — Julian Savulescu. **Notes:** The original text was a close paraphrase of the Principle of Procreative Beneficence. It has been corrected to the exact definition provided by the author in the source article.

[71] *Each one of us was harmed by being brought into existence.* — David Benatar. **Notes:** The original text is an accurate summary of the book's thesis, but not a direct quote. Corrected to the first sentence of the book's introduction.

[72] *...a fetus is not a person, and hence not the sort of entity...* — Mary Anne Warren. **Notes:** The original text is a thematic summary of a legal principle, but it is not a direct quote from this specific philosophical essay. Corrected to an actual quote from the work.

[73] *Self-knowledge through numbers.* — Gary Wolf & Kevin K.... **Notes:** The original text combines the movement's tagline with a descriptive summary. Corrected to the exact tagline.

[74] *When we constantly track our reproductive health, our identi...* — Netflix. **Notes:** Could not be verified. The provided source does not appear to cover the topic of fertility tracking, and the user's notes describe the text as a 'thematic summary,' not a direct quote.

synapse traces

[75] *Although gamification can be a powerful tool to engage users...* — Sardi L, Idri A, Fer.... **Notes:** The original text is a plausible application of the paper's findings to fertility, but it is not a direct quote and the paper does not specifically discuss fertility. Corrected to an actual quote from the article.

[76] *The promise of the Quantified Self is that the data will mak...* — Gideon Lewis-Kraus. **Notes:** The original text is an accurate thematic summary but not a direct quote from the article. Corrected to an actual quote and updated the author from the general publication to the specific writer.

[77] *Many Americans turn to online sources and social media for h...* — Pew Research Center. **Notes:** The original text is a thematic summary of the report's findings applied to a specific context, but it is not a direct quote from the source. Corrected to a general quote from the report's overview.

[78] *Surveillance capitalism unilaterally claims human experience...* — Shoshana Zuboff. **Notes:** The original text is an excellent summary of a key theme but is not a direct quote. Corrected to a foundational definition from the book's introduction.

[79] *The ability to process all the data of an individual and pro...* — Eric Topol. **Notes:** The original text accurately summarizes a key argument of the book but is not a direct quote. Corrected to an actual quote from the book on a similar theme.

[80] *Automation bias is the tendency to over-rely on automated ai...* — Lyell D, Coiera E, C.... **Notes:** The original text is an accurate summary of the article's main point but is not a direct quote. Corrected to the article's definition of automation bias and updated the author format.

[81] *Family planning decisions are deeply emotional. While an AI ...* — Roland T. Rust & Mi.... **Notes:** Could not be verified with available tools. The quote reflects themes present in the book but does not appear to be a direct quotation.

[82] *The question of who is responsible when something goes wrong...* — European Parliament. **Notes:** Original was a paraphrase of the

document's central themes. Corrected to a direct quote from the source and updated the source's title.

[83] *For some, these tools are a way to outsource the emotional l...* — Tanya Basu. **Notes:** Original quote could not be verified in the source article. It appears to be a summary of the article's ideas. Replaced with an authentic quote and corrected the source title and author.

[84] *When we outsource our memory to a machine, we also outsource...* — Nicholas Carr. **Notes:** Original quote is an application of the author's ideas to a specific topic, not a direct quote from the book. Replaced with an authentic quote on a similar theme.

[85] *Nutrigenomics explores how specific foods and nutrients inte...* — National Institutes .... **Notes:** Could not be verified with available tools. The quote appears to combine a general definition of nutrigenomics with a separate statement about biohackers and is not found in NIH publications.

[86] *You can't manage what you don't measure, and that is especia...* — Dave Asprey. **Notes:** Original quote is a summary of the author's ideas, not a direct quote. The source title was also incorrect. Replaced with an authentic quote from the correct book.

[87] *The use of nootropics (cognitive enhancers) and various supp...* — Elise Bohan. **Notes:** Could not be verified with available tools. The quote does not appear in the author's known works, and the provided source title appears to be incorrect.

[88] *Knowing your carrier status can empower you with important i...* — 23andMe, Inc.. **Notes:** Original was an accurate summary of the website's content, not a direct quote. Replaced with an authentic quote from the 23andMe website.

[89] *Biohacking is a form of citizen science that takes place out...* — Alessandro Delfanti. **Notes:** Original quote is an accurate summary of the book's themes but is not a direct quote. Replaced with an authentic quote from the book's introduction.

[90] *Biohacking communities, often organized online, function as ...* — Mary Ellen Hannibal. **Notes:** Could not be verified with available

tools. The quote is misattributed; the cited book focuses on broader citizen science and does not contain this text about biohacking.

Family Support: Data vs. Intuition

synapse traces

Bibliography

(NIH), National Institutes of Health. Nutrigenomics and the Future of Nutrition. New York: National Academies Press, 2016.

(translator), B. Ebbell. The Papyrus Ebers: The Greatest Egyptian Medical Document. New York: Unknown Publisher, 1991.

Adams, J. R. G.. Queering the Quantified Self: An Intersectional Approach to Health-Tracking Technologies. New York: Unknown Publisher, 2022.

Mohammed Abdullah Al-Marridi, Mohammed S. Al-Kahtani, Wadha Abdullah Al-Marridi, and Abdulla Al-Marridi. Health and Fitness App Data Breaches: A Scoping Review. New York: Unknown Publisher, 2021.

Almeling, Rene. The Business of Fertility: How 'Femtech' Is (and Is Not) Disrupting Reproduction. New York: Routledge, 2020.

Asprey, Dave. Super Human: The Bulletproof Plan to Age Backward and Maybe Even Live Forever. New York: HarperCollins, 2019.

Association, American Humanist. Humanist Manifesto III. New York: Unitarian Universalist Association of Congregations, 2003.

Atwood, Margaret. The Handmaid's Tale. New York: McClelland Stewart, 1985.

Banks, Iain M.. Excession. New York: Orbit, 1987.

Basu, Tanya. Meet the people using AI to make their relationships better. New York: Unknown Publisher, 2021.

Benatar, David. Better Never to Have Been: The Harm of Coming into Existence. New York: OUP Oxford, 2006.

Benson, Herbert. The Relaxation Response. New York: Harmony, 1975.

Bohan, Elise. Hacking the Human: The Rise of Biohacking and the Future of Health. New York: Muzaffar Munshi, 2022.

Bombardieri, Merle. The Baby Decision: How to Make the Most Important Choice of Your Life. New York: Unknown Publisher, 1981.

Carr, Nicholas. The Glass Cage: Automation and Us. New York: National Geographic Books, 2014.

Center, Pew Research. Sharing and Obscuring Personal Health Information on Social Media. New York: IGI Global, 2019.

Sara Gerke, Timo Minssen
I. Glenn Cohen. The need for a system-level regulatory framework for artificial intelligence in medicine. New York: Springer Nature, 2020.

Conrad, Peter. The Medicalization of Society: On the Transformation of Human Conditions into Treatable Disorders. New York: Arkose Press, 2007.

Court, U.S. Supreme. Griswold v. Connecticut, 381 U.S. 479. New York: Unknown Publisher, 1965.

Delfanti, Alessandro. Biohackers: The Politics of Open Science. New York: Pluto Books, 2013.

Dworkin, Ronald. Life's Dominion: An Argument About Abortion, Euthanasia, and Individual Freedom. New York: Vintage, 1993.

Eig, Jonathan. The Birth of the Pill: How Four Crusaders Reinvented Sex and Launched a Revolution. New York: Everest Media LLC, 2014.

Engelman, Peter C.. A History of the Birth Control Movement in America. New York: Bloomsbury Publishing USA, 2011.

Forum, World Economic. Femtech: A new frontier for women's health or a new way to exploit their data?. New York: John Wiley Sons, 2023.

Foundation, Electronic Frontier. Security and Privacy Tips for People Seeking an Abortion. New York: Unknown Publisher, 2022.

Hannibal, Mary Ellen. The Citizen Scientist: A New Way to Engage in Discovery. New York: Unknown Publisher, 2016.

Harvey, Peter. An Introduction to Buddhist Ethics: Foundations, Values and Issues. New York: Cambridge University Press, 2000.

Hendrickson-Jack, Lisa. The Fifth Vital Sign: Master Your Cycles Optimize Your Fertility. New York: Fertility Friday Publishing Inc., 2019.

Hochschild, Arlie Russell. The Managed Heart: Commercialization of Human Feeling. New York: Univ of California Press, 1983.

Hopkins, Thomas J.. The Hindu Religious Tradition. New York: Unknown Publisher, 1971.

Huang, Roland T. Rust Ming-Hui. The Feeling Economy: How Artificial Intelligence is Creating the Era of Empathy. New York: Springer Nature, 2021.

Huxley, Aldous. Brave New World. New York: Harper Collins, 1932.

23andMe, Inc.. 23andMe Website. New York: Unknown Publisher, 2006.

Institution, Brookings. The 'black box' problem: A lack of transparency in AI decision-making. New York: Independently Published, 2020.

Ishiguro, Kazuo. Never Let Me Go. New York: Vintage, 2005.

Sardi L, Idri A, Fernández-Alemán JL. Gamification in Health and Wellness: A Systematic Review of the Literature. New York: IGI Global, 2017.

Jensen, Jill Petigara Lynn. Yoga and Fertility: A Journey to Health and Healing. New York: Demos Medical Publishing, 2006.

Kelly, Gary Wolf Kevin. Quantified Self Website. New York: John Wiley Sons, 2010.

Kimmerer, Robin Wall. Braiding Sweetgrass: Indigenous Wisdom, Scientific Knowledge and the Teachings of Plants. New York: Milkweed Editions, 2013.

Knight, Jane. The Complete Guide to Fertility Awareness. New York: Taylor Francis, 2016.

Lewis-Kraus, Gideon. The Data-Driven Life. New York: Independently Published, 2014.

Michaels, Susan J. Douglas and Meredith W.. The Mommy Myth: The Idealization of Motherhood and How It Has Undermined Women. New York: Simon and Schuster, 2004.

Solon Barocas, Moritz Hardt, Arvind Narayanan. Fairness and Machine Learning: Limitations and Opportunities. New York: MIT Press, 2019.

Netflix. The Goop Lab (Season 1, Episode 5). New York: Unknown Publisher, 2020.

Niccol, Andrew. Gattaca. New York: Cambridge University Press, 1997.

Northrup, Christiane. Women's Bodies, Women's Wisdom: Creating Physical and Emotional Health and Healing. New York: Hay House, Inc, 1994.

Organization, World Health. Ethics and governance of artificial intelligence for health. New York: World Health Organization, 2021.

Organization, World Health. Family Planning: A Global Handbook for Providers (2018 edition). New York: Unknown Publisher, 2018.

Parliament, European. Responsible AI: A legal and ethical analysis. New York: Springer Nature, 2020.

I. Glenn Cohen, Eli Y. Adashi
Vardit Ravitsky. The Ethics of AI in Reproductive Medicine: A Call for a Deliberative Approach. New York: Springer, 2021.

Rienzi, Antonio Capalbo
Laura. The role of artificial intelligence in preimplantation genetic testing. New York: Springer Nature, 2021.

Robertson, John A.. The Right to Procreate. New York: Princeton University Press, 1983.

Ross, Casey. Widely used algorithm for hospital admissions is racially biased, study finds. New York: Unknown Publisher, 2019.

Perski, O., Naughton, F., Garnett, C., Blandford, A., West, R., Michie, S.. User Engagement in Digital Health Interventions: A Systematic Review of Reviews. New York: Unknown Publisher,

2017.

Sanders, Rebecca G. Simmons Laura M.. Digital-Health Apps for Fertility and Contraception: A Review of the Evidence. New York: Unknown Publisher, 2021.

Sanger, Margaret. Woman and the New Race. New York: CreateSpace, 1920.

Savulescu, Julian. Procreative Beneficence: Why We Should Select the Best Children. New York: OUP Oxford, 2001.

Sender, Katherine. Digital Infertilities: The Social Construction of Technology and the Body in Online Fertility Communities. New York: Springer, 2019.

Steinbock, Bonnie. The Limits of Procreative Liberty. New York: Unknown Publisher, 1994.

Steptoe, Robert Edwards Patrick. A Matter of Life: The Story of a Medical Breakthrough. New York: Unknown Publisher, 1980.

Matthias Doepke, Anne Hannusch, Fabian Kindermann, and Michèle Tertilt. The New Economics of Fertility. New York: Unknown Publisher, 2022.

Topol, Eric. The Patient Will See You Now: The Future of Medicine is in Your Hands. New York: Unknown Publisher, 2015.

Topol, Eric. Deep Medicine: How Artificial Intelligence Can Make Healthcare Human Again. New York: Basic Books, 2019.

International Islamic Centre for Population Studies and Research, Al-Azhar University. Islam and Family Planning. New York: Routledge, 1995.

Various. The Bible (English Standard Version). New York: Unknown Publisher, -1400.

Walker, Ellen L.. Complete Without Kids: An Insider's Guide to Childfree Living by Choice. New York: Greenleaf Book Group, 2011.

Warren, Mary Anne. On the Moral and Legal Status of Abortion. New York: Unknown Publisher, 1973.

Marcos Meseguer, Antonio M. García-Velasco Dagan Wells. Artificial intelligence in the IVF laboratory: a review of the literature and a future vision. New York: Elsevier, 2021.

Wells, H.G.. The Island of Doctor Moreau. New York: Graphic Arts Books, 1896.

Weschler, Toni. Taking Charge of Your Fertility, 20th Anniversary Edition. New York: William Morrow Paperbacks, 1995.

Westmore, Evelyn Billings Ann. The Billings Method: Controlling Fertility without Drugs or Devices. New York: Gracewing Publishing, 1980.

Zaretsky, Eli. Capitalism, the Family, and Personal Life. New York: Verso Books, 1976.

Zuboff, Shoshana. The Age of Surveillance Capitalism: The Fight for a Human Future at the New Frontier of Power. New York: PublicAffairs, 2019.

al., Milad Vazan et. A review on machine learning approaches for prediction of pregnancy-related outcomes from assisted reproductive technology. New York: MIT Press, 2022.

al., Shac-Lee Lim et. Wearable sensors for assessing the reproductive cycle: a scoping review. New York: MDPI, 2023.

al., Chelsea B. Polis et. Evaluation of the accuracy of fertility awareness-based method apps. New York: Unknown Publisher, 2023.

al., Deborah A. Levine et. The Quantified Self in Preconception Care: A Qualitative Study of Fertility Tracking App Users. New York: John Wiley Sons, 2021.

al., Emre Seli et. Big data and artificial intelligence: a new era for reproductive medicine. New York: Springer Nature, 2022.

al., Edgardo Somigliana et. Personalized medicine in human reproduction: a proposal for a patient-centered approach. New York: Springer Nature, 2021.

al., Angela Lu et. The Use of Chatbots in Reproductive Health: A Scoping Review. New York: IGI Global, 2023.

al., Signe N. Stelling et. The role of telehealth in reproductive medicine during the COVID-19 pandemic and beyond. New York: Frontiers

Media SA, 2021.

al., Dominik G. Grimm et. Nudging in health and healthcare: a systematic review of the literature. New York: National Academies Press, 2023.

al., Sarah Rosenfeld et. Privacy policies of Android diabetes apps and sharing of health information. New York: IGI Global, 2019.

Cirillo, D., Catuara-Solarz, S., Morey, C., et al.. Algorithmic Bias in Health Care: A Systematic Review. New York: Academic Press, 2020.

al., U. E. E. Ofondu et. The digital divide in health and healthcare: A commentary. New York: National Academies Press, 2022.

al., L M Blank et. Development and validation of a machine learning model for prediction of live birth after in vitro fertilization. New York: Unknown Publisher, 2022.

al., M. C. Maggiulli et. Robotics in the reproductive medicine laboratory: A new era. New York: Academic Press, 2020.

al., Robert A. Hatcher et. Contraceptive Technology, 21st Edition. New York: Unknown Publisher, 1971.

al., Martha O. Diamond et. Unsung Lullabies: Understanding and Coping with Infertility. New York: Macmillan + ORM, 2005.

Lyell D, Coiera E, Chen J, et al.. The risks of automation bias in medical decision-making. New York: Rand Corporation, 2021.

Family Support: Data vs. Intuition

synapse traces

For more information and to purchase this book, please visit our website:

NimbleBooks.com

Family Support: Data vs. Intuition

www.ingramcontent.com/pod-product-compliance
Lightning Source LLC
Chambersburg PA
CBHW040309170426
43195CB00020B/2908